W9-BDU-155

REMBRANDT VAN RIJN

REMBRANDT

Diane Kelder

Department of Art History

Finch College

McGRAW-HILL BOOK COMPANY · NEW YORK·LONDON·TORONTO·SYDNEY

Copyright © 1970 by McGraw-Hill, Inc. All rights reserved. Printed in the United States of America. Slides manufactured by Scala, Florence. No part of this publication may be reproduced, stored in a retrieval system, or transmitted, in any form or by any means, electronic, mechanical, photocopying, recording, or otherwise, without prior written permission of the publisher. Library of Congress Catalog Card Number: 74-92727   33442

Cover picture. *Self-Portrait in Studio Attire,* drawing, 8″ x 5¾″ Rembrandtshuis, Amsterdam.

THE GREATEST PAINTER of seventeenth-century Holland, and one of the outstanding natural geniuses in the history of European art, Rembrandt van Rijn was a generation younger than Rubens and the contemporary of Van Dyck and Velásquez. He produced neither a great body of influential theoretical writings as did Leonardo da Vinci, nor was he as universally acclaimed by his contemporaries as were Michelangelo and Raphael. Nevertheless, he impressed his stamp of genius on a generation of Dutch painters and served to spark the imaginations of countless eighteenth- and nineteenth-century artists.

Rembrandt's output was enormous, and the more than two thousand works that have survived in the three hundred years since his death testify to the breadth of his vision, his immense technical skill in every medium—oil, drawing, etching—and the remarkable durability of his artistic message. From studying and portraying his own character, as shown in the many self-portraits that he painted throughout his life, he turned to a careful study of others, never forgetting that his subjects were human and never losing the compassion that was the result of wide, personal experience. His emotions extended from exhilaration and boundless optimism to profound despair; his range of acquaintances was as wide as his gaze; and his memory apparently long enough to always recall with affection the homely pleasures of his youth even while enjoying the fruits of professional success.

Eminently successful in his earlier years, Rembrandt later encountered severe personal misfortunes accompanied by a notable decline in the popularity of his work in his native Holland. In the early eighteenth century, when the Dutch art historian and critic Arnold Houbraken compiled his *Great Theater of Netherlandish Artists,* the profile of Rembrandt was sketchy and somewhat biased. In addition to contributing some rather serious misinformation about Rembrandt's life, Houbraken's thesis continued to spread tales that had been invented by the painter's contemporaries alluding to unsupported evidence of his miserliness, clumsiness, and irascibility. Houbraken also perpetuated the legend, first proposed by Joachim von Sandrart, a German artist known for his history and portraits of Dutch nobility, that Rembrandt was unlettered, uncouth, and consorted with lowly or vulgar people. But though Rembrandt, unlike Rubens, left no substantial number of chatty letters,

Frontispiece.
Self-Portait (1640)
oil on canvas, 38¼" x 31⅛"
The National Gallery, London

[Facing this page]
Detail of Figure 15

the extant correspondence does reveal him to have been poised, serious, and quite literate. Indeed, the relative smallness of Rembrandt's correspondence cannot possibly be construed as an indication of his intellectual limitations, for if such criteria were valid, we would have to indict a vast number of most distinguished artists.

Rembrandt did continue to maintain a strong international reputation during his lifetime, and he never ceased to be a productive and popular artist. But it was during the late eighteenth and early nineteenth centuries, with the birth of Romanticism, that the individualism of his life and work was reevaluated, became ever more appealing to artists and historians, and generated an interest in this most creative painter, etcher, and draftsman that is not easily surpassed today.

Rembrandt was born in the small university town of Leyden on July 14, 1606, the fifth of six children. His father, Harmen Gerritsz van Rijn, whose family came from the region near the Rhine river, was a fairly well-to-do miller; his mother, Cornelia, the daughter of a baker. Politically, the years of Rembrandt's childhood were unusually calm and peaceful. Early in the seventeenth century, Holland, or the United Provinces, had emerged as an independent colonial power and had entered a period of great commercial prosperity. The country's considerable seapower helped to create a sphere of economic interest that extended from continental Europe to the South Pacific. Within a short time, this overseas expansion had generated an atmosphere of affluence, vitality, and optimism which proved most beneficial to the fine arts.

In Holland the traditional sources of art patronage—the Church and the aristocracy—became increasingly less active. Only a small number of paintings were commissioned by the royal family. Also, the resounding success of the Reformation brought a drastic reduction in the number of Catholics and, since the Calvinist church did not patronize the fine arts, that source of patronage quickly disappeared. But for most Dutch artists the lack of organized patronage posed no serious problem; in the wealthy burgher class there were thousands of potential patrons eager to employ them.

In a sense, the career of Rembrandt reflects the various phases of political, economic, and social development in seventeenth-century Holland. During the artist's youth, the exuberant, impressionistic style of Frans Hals (1580?-1666) dominated Dutch painting. Hals, with his extraordinary vivacity and bold good humor, expressed little concern for the spiritual in man, but focused instead on man's delight in the pleasures of the senses and the joys of contemporary life. His paintings accurately reflect the first phase of seventeenth-century Dutch history and the predilection of the middle class for subjects which echoed the peace and prosperity they had created and now wished to enjoy. Later, in the sixties, when Holland unsuccessfully challenged England's maritime supremacy, her prosperity markedly declined. The French invasion by Louis XIV in 1672, although checked, robbed Holland's vitality, and her seemingly unlimited optimism gave way to a period of sober introspection.

Nowhere is the record of this change in attitude more clearly documented than in the self-portraits which Rembrandt executed almost continually from the 1620s until his death in 1669. The sixty oil paintings, numerous drawings and etchings reveal not only the gradual maturing of his artistic vision, but provide an intimate testimony of his varying moods and psychological states. Seldom did a year of the artist's life pass without his having drawn or painted a record of his appearance and humor. These self-portraits almost constitute a total view of the artist, demonstrating his frank, and often merciless, power of observation and his amazing gift for capturing the essence of a mood and translating it into a meaningful visual statement. Both in quantity and in quality the self-portraits of Rembrandt are more significant than those of any other artist (with the possible exception of his countryman Vincent van Gogh), and none has left us with such comparably affecting personal statements. Like many other artists Rembrandt may have started painting his own likeness because it provided a cheap, convenient model for developing a repertory of facial expressions. Yet this is surely only a partial explanation of the painter's virtually obsessive concern with the recording of his features. It is far more likely that he was inclined to use this introspection as a point of departure toward the comprehension of others, for in better understanding himself he grew more sensitive to others.

A tiny etching, done when he was twenty-four, reveals how Rembrandt tried to catch the essence of a fleeting emotion (Figure 1). His somewhat coarse features are distorted by surprise or astonishment, his eyes fixed in fear, the disheveled hair and raised shoulder suggesting a sudden withdrawal from something quite unexpected. This etching dates from the artist's earliest period (1621-1626), those years he spent working in his native city of Leyden with Jacob Isaaksz van Swanenburgh and, later, in Amsterdam, with Pieter Lastman. Rembrandt entered Swanenburgh's studio as a boy of fifteen, and remained with the minor artist about three years before continuing his studies with the more accomplished and celebrated Lastman.

Figure 1.
Self-Portrait in a Cap, Open-mouthed and Staring
(1630) etching, 2½" x 2"

However, before he reached his decision to become a painter, Rembrandt spent a few short months at the University of Leyden. Probably he did so in order to please his parents. Although uneducated people of modestly comfortable means, they apparently had ambitions for their gifted young son. Like many middle-class Hollanders, they respected learning and culture and wished to see their son enjoy the benefits that derived from a gentleman's humanistic education. Accordingly, the seven-year-old Rembrandt was sent to Leyden's Latin School, where he remained for several years. The school's course of study included a fairly thorough grounding in grammar and classical literature, as well as a careful consideration of appropriate religious texts. This educational experience does not seem to have had a profound effect on Rembrandt, for it is difficult to point to persistent and significant intellectual concerns in his work. Among his paintings there are subjects taken from classical

Figure 2.
The Three Trees (1643)
etching, 8¼″ x 11″

sources, notably Ovid's *Metamorphoses,* but, like all his narratives, they adhere fairly closely to the text. Unlike so many other Northern artists (Rubens, Van Dyck, Honthorst, Terbrugghen, his teacher Lastman), Rembrandt never journeyed to Italy to view the great ruins of classical antiquity or to pay homage to the masterpieces of the Italian Renaissance. He seems rather to have drawn constant and direct inspiration from the daily sights of his native Holland, from the vigor of her people, and from the somewhat melancholy beauty of her landscape (Figure 2).

Although Rembrandt studied with Swanenburgh for three years, there is really no trace of that master's influence on his work. The first really important artistic impact was made by Pieter Lastman, with whom he worked in Amsterdam between 1624-1625. In Lastman the young painter found a subtler, more sophisticated sensibility than that of the provincial Swanenburgh. Lastman made a particularly important contribution to the young Rembrandt's development by introducing him to the painting of historical and biblical subjects. Moreover, in Lastman, a robust and imaginative painter with a love of the dramatic and exotic, the pupil found a kindred spirit; he quickly absorbed his teacher's taste for theatricality, and transformed it into a dashing style of his own.

The student of a Dutch Mannerist, Lastman had visited Rome early in the century at a time when the dramatic lighting innovations of Caravaggio and the eclectic classicism of Annibale Carracci were exerting considerable influence. Many of the Northern painters seized upon the new realism and chiaroscuro of Caravaggio and adapted his style to a particularly Dutch concern for narrative and anecdote.

Rembrandt in his formative years was fascinated by these Northern artists and influenced by works such as Terbrugghen's version of *The Calling of St. Matthew* (Figure 3), a richer, brighter, and busier work than Caravaggio's starkly dramatic telling of the religious story. At twenty-one Rembrandt painted *The Moneychanger,* a secular work which utilizes details from Terbrugghen's work, as well as its chiaroscuro (Figure 4).

After his brief sojourn in Amsterdam, Rembrandt returned to Leyden and remained there until 1631. Comparatively little historical documentation exists of this period of his life, but the paintings reveal something of its experience and artistic limitations. A large number of the works produced are portraits of members of his family—mother, father, sister—and the inevitable self-portraits. There is a fascination with exotic or romantic figure types, often shown in Oriental or quasi-Oriental costumes, with turbans and lavish silks, that reveals the influence of Lastman as the young painter gropes toward an independent style. Some of this early love of the rich and theatrical might also be traced to the presence of numerous university students and teachers from central and eastern Europe, whose dress surely differed from that of the Leyden locals.

Often Rembrandt transcended his initial concern for facial expression, figure placement, and splendid costumes to produce a moving and penetrating expression of personal sentiment, such as the portrait of his mother in the guise of the Hebrew prophetess Hannah tracing the letters of her holy book (Figure 5). Rembrandt's portraits of his mother—

9

Figure 3.
Hendrik Terbrugghen (1588-1629)
The Calling of St. Matthew
oil on canvas, 60" x 76¾"
Musée des Beaux-Arts, Le Havre

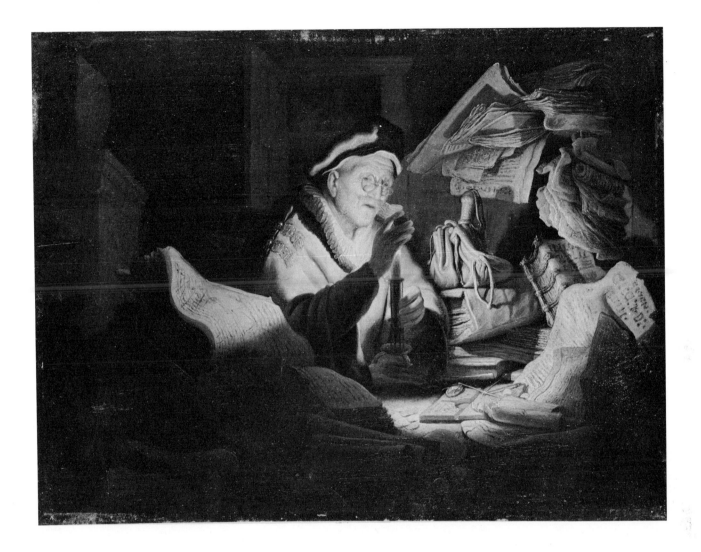

Figure 4.
The Moneychanger (1627)
oil on panel, 12½″ x 16½″
Staaliche Museen, Berlin-Dahlem

apart from revealing his deep love for her and empathy with her simple, genuine piety —shed light on one very important aspect of his character: affection for and understanding of elderly people, whom he represents with gentle dignity and solemnity as if the face of age were a metaphor for human wisdom. Throughout his life the painter maintained this appreciation of the poignant vulnerability and contemplative quality associated with old age. This sensitivity sustained him well, especially in the last years of his life when his own infirmities and personal tragedies seemed insupportable.

Rembrandt must have enjoyed considerable success in his hometown, for we know that he had a number of gifted pupils by the time he again left Leyden for Amsterdam in 1631. No doubt his move to that city was prompted by a taste of success and the promise of even greater recognition and financial reward in the thriving, art-conscious capital. Amsterdam was one of the busiest and wealthiest cities in the world, with a heterogeneous and sophisticated population. Many of the city's residents were foreign merchants who contributed to the impression of cosmopolitanism, and who supported cultural activities such as its lively theater.

The ambitious young painter formed a business partnership with the art dealer and painter Hendrik van Uylenburgh, which allowed him to live in the latter's elegant town house. In a short time Rembrandt, with van Uylenburgh's counsel, became one of Amsterdam's most sought after portrait painters. Foremost among the works which helped to build Rembrandt's reputation was his first large group portrait, the *Anatomy Lesson of Doctor Nicolaas Tulp* (Slide 2), commissioned by the Guild of Surgeons in 1632. The earliest of Rembrandt's great "corporation" portraits, it preceded *The Night Watch* (Slide 10) by ten years and the *Syndics of the Drapers' Guild* (Slide 19) by thirty. Each painting marks a significant moment in his career. At the time of the *Anatomy Lesson* Rembrandt was still testing and developing his descriptive skills, and struggling to master problems of composition such as the establishment of spatial relationships, the accentuation of narrative and dramatic elements through effective, controlled lighting, and the creation of systematically related tonal values. Rembrandt's contemporaries must have considered his achievement quite remarkable, for previous representations of anatomy lessons appear static and clumsily posed by comparison. To paint a corpse as such was a rare opportunity, and the entire work proved an unusual challenge for a young artist with a quickly developing taste for naturalism and visual truth.

The *Anatomy Lesson* signaled the beginning of a period of extraordinary public acclaim, as well as a decade of great prosperity and personal happiness. In 1632 Rembrandt married Saskia van Uylenburgh, the cousin of his partner and the daughter of a well-to-do and much respected burgomaster of Leeuwarden, a town near Amsterdam. With his marriage to Saskia, whose family was considered patrician, the painter's social status was elevated considerably and he was able to greatly increase his contacts with the wealthy patrons of Amsterdam. Not only was he sought after as a painter of fashionable portraits, but students began to flock to his studio and pay high prices for the opportunity of learning his secrets.

Rembrandt apparently adored his wife. He painted or drew her likeness over and over, sometimes depicting her as a mythological personage, her handsome but robust face only slightly idealized, her costumes always extremely elegant. Sir Kenneth Clark has remarked more generally of Rembrandt's mythological portraits: "The trappings, belonging to the world of fantasy, are indeed a display of mannerist accomplishment. The persons belong to the world of experience—not simply visual experience, but daily human contact—and are represented without any mitigation which might bring their homely features into harmony with their splendid accoutrements."

No doubt Saskia served generally as the feminine ideal for many paintings done before her death in 1642. The couple's happy life together is documented in several double portraits of which the one from the late 1630s is the most flamboyant (Figure 6). The richness of the costumes, the obvious allusions to good living and the pleasures of the table, and the suggestive bravado of the poses reveal Rembrandt at his most extravagant. It is tempting to think of this work as a reflection of the painter's self-satisfaction at having passed from promising young artist to accomplished and acclaimed master in a breathtakingly short span

Figure 5.
Rembrandt's Mother as the Prophetess Hannah (1631)
oil on panel, 23⅝" x 18¾"
Rijksmuseum, Amsterdam

of time. Moreover, one cannot help but think of the change in his standard of living from the modest but comfortable life in Leyden to the splendor of housekeeping in Amsterdam. Scholars have pointed out that the pose of the figures recalls the parable of the Prodigal Son who indulged in sensual pleasure before his downfall. Later in his career, Rembrandt was to use this affecting story in some of his most eloquent works.

In the midst of his greatest material prosperity, Rembrandt found time to undertake a number of religious paintings. An important commission for Prince Frederick Henry of Orange, a series of canvases illustrating the Passion of Christ, probably came to Rembrandt through the good offices of Constantin Huygens, who was first taken with the artist's work when he visited Leyden in 1629. Huygens, in addition to serving the princes of Orange, was a man of letters and art connoisseur whose correspondents included such distinguished contemporaries as Pierre Corneille and René Descartes. In the course of the 1630s Rembrandt wrote Huygens a number of letters which reflect the practical concerns of the Passion series, but also reveal his quest for spiritual as well as visual truth. Trying to explain why it had taken him so long to complete the *Entombment* and *Resurrection,* although the *Elevation* and *Descent from the Cross* (Slide 3) were finished by 1633, Rembrandt tells Huygens that he has attempted to express "the greatest and most inward emotion." Emotion is certainly the hallmark of the Passion series, as it is of so many of his religious subjects, for Rembrandt's religious faith, doubtless shaped by his mother's piety, was deep and sincere. To Rembrandt, the figure of Christ was not the authoritarian Judge of his fellow Calvinists, but a loving, understanding, and human figure whose compassion and love were for all men and all times. He shared, however, the Calvinist love of the Old Testament and, as a gesture of thanks to Huygens, painted a large *Blinding of Samson* (Slide 6). The violence and drama of the story are typically Baroque, but especially relevant for Huygens and all Rembrandt's countrymen was the figure of Samson, the Jewish champion who had vanquished the oppressive Philistines. With memories of their struggle for independence still vivid, the Dutch found his story particularly meaningful.

Rembrandt constantly indulged his newly acquired and expensive tastes during the ten years of his marriage to Saskia. Unlike those artists who anticipated a possible decline in their popularity and prudently set aside sums of money for their old age, Rembrandt was a lavish spender. He enjoyed the pleasures of a good table and ran his household on a grand scale. Saskia's fortune and the princely sums he received for his paintings enabled him to indulge his taste for collecting *objets d'art.* From reports of the late seventeenth-century Italian critic and art historian Filippo Baldinucci, we know that Rembrandt haunted public auctions and bought great quantities of old-fashioned, somewhat theatrical clothes which he hung in his studio along with ". . . arrows, halberds, daggers, sabers, knives, and so on—and innumerable quantities of drawings, engravings, and medals, and every other thing which he thought a painter might need." Baldinucci also relates that Rembrandt was such a high bidder at these auctions that other potential buyers were intimidated; the painter explained his conduct by saying he wished to enhance the prestige of his profession.

Figure 6.
Double Portrait of Rembrandt and Saskia (1636)
oil on canvas, 63¼" x 51½"
Staatliche Kunstsammlungen
Dresden

15

Figure 7.
Man on Horseback
(1654-1656)
(after an Indian miniature)
pen and bistre with washes
in watercolor
8⅛″ x 7″
The British Museum, London

Figure 8.
Baldassare Castiglione
(1639)
(after Raphael)
pen, bistre, and some
white body color
6⅜″ x 8⅛″
Graphische Sammlung Albertina
Vienna

Figure 9.
Baby Learning to Walk
black chalk, 4″ x 5″
The British Museum
London

Figure 10.
*Three Elephants
and their Keeper*
(c.1637)
black chalk
9½″ x 14⅜″
Graphische Sammlung Albertina
Vienna

In 1639 Rembrandt purchased a large and handsome house on a fashionable street. Apparently the price of the house was substantial, for it severely taxed his available funds and left him in a very precarious financial condition. The house, on the Joden-Breestraat, was to serve as a museum for Rembrandt's growing collection of paintings, drawings, prints, and other treasures. An inventory made in 1656, when the painter was forced to declare bankruptcy, includes an extraordinary list of paintings. There were, of course, many of Rembrandt's own works, but also a considerable number by earlier Italian and Flemish painters as well as contemporary Dutch masters: Raphael, Palma Vecchio, Giorgione, Jacopo Bassano, Lelio Orsi, Jan van Eyck, Lucas van Leyden, Adriaen Brouwer, Jan Lievens, Hercules Seghers, and his teacher Lastman. Also inventoried was ancient sculpture in the form of originals and plaster copies, some examples of Oriental art, and a rather small number of books. If as a student the young Rembrandt did not serve an apprentice's homage to the monuments of Italy's past, his appreciation and quest for works of art from distant times and places proved to be both sensitive and expensive. Several copies he made of Indian miniatures reveal how well he understood the calligraphic and coloristic nuances of the Oriental draftsman (Figure 7). Executed in light pen and wash, these studies manage to capture the essence of the delicate movement implicit in the originals. In addition, they also served the very practical function of providing models for Rembrandt's numerous exotic figure types.

Rembrandt never ceased to collect, and to copy, admired originals although his financial collapse was to drastically curtail his acquisitions. When the dealer Lucas van Uffelen brought Raphael's portrait of the Renaissance man of letters Count Baldassare Castiglione to Amsterdam in 1639 and sold it at auction, Rembrandt was there. He made a quick sketch of the work, noting its title and auction price of 3500 guilders (Figure 8). Later he adapted the pose of Raphael's famous sitter in an etched self-portrait, and the following year he reversed it in an oil painting (Frontispiece). During the late thirties Rembrandt also made several drawings after copies of Leonardo's *Last Supper.* In a perceptive study of Rembrandt's use of Italian Renaissance sources, Sir Kenneth Clark noted the eagerness to master the principles of design, and suggested that Rembrandt's numerous copies of famous earlier works served not only to fix these compositions in his memory, but to help him perfect techniques.

Rembrandt was easily the greatest draftsman of the seventeenth century and probably one of the greatest of all time. His drawings served a number of purposes: many were used, as the copy of the Indian miniature attests, to preserve the likeness of an admired original; countless others provided the basic elements for a projected oil painting. Some were partial preparation for the artist's many etchings, while a large group simply recorded Rembrandt's spontaneous reaction to such ordinary human events as a baby's first steps (Figure 9). His remarkable naturalism is never keener than in the numerous pen or chalk sketches such as the rare and wonderful studies of animals (Figure 10). Most of the works are surprisingly

Figure 11.
*A Sheet of Studies
with Nine Different Heads
and Half-length Figures* (c.1636)
pen, wash and red chalk, 8¾″ x 9″
Barber Institute of Fine Arts
University of Birmingham

small and were doubtless kept in a portfolio to which Rembrandt's pupils had access. There, arranged according to subject matter, they constituted a vast repertory of types, attitudes, and facial expressions which students used for reference (Figure 11). Rembrandt valued his own drawings as he valued the drawings of others. While most of his art collection was liquidated by auction following his bankruptcy in 1656, his holdings in "Papier Kunst" were so large that a special sale had to be arranged two years later.

In his definitive study of Rembrandt's drawings, Otto Benesch points out that the artist's drawings were extremely popular with collectors during the seventeenth century. By the early eighteenth century, the Dutch critic Arnold Houbraken wrote of Rembrandt's pen drawings:

> . . . the emotions of the soul caused by different events are seen so artistically and clearly in their essential features that it is a marvel to look at — anger, grief, hatred, joy, and so on; everything is delineated so naturally that one can read in the pen-strokes what each one wants to say.

One Rembrandt pupil, Govaert Flinck, managed to assemble an important group of drawings, which subsequently were acquired by the Duke of Devonshire, and now con-

Figure 12.
Saint Augustine in his Study
(c.1635-1636)
pen and bistre
7¼″ x 5⅞″
Collection of the
Duke of Devonshire
Chatsworth

Figure 13.
Portrait of Rembrandt's Mother (1628)
etching, 3½″ x 2¾″
Metropolitan Museum of Art, New York,
Rogers Fund, 1918

Figure 14.
View of Amsterdam (1640)
etching, 4⅜″ x 6″

stitute a goodly part of his famous Chatsworth collection. A drawing, possibly representing Saint Augustine (Figure 12), provides a typical example of a subject that fascinated Rembrandt—the elderly, isolated, contemplative scholar searching for truth and the meaning of human experience. Quick but telling lines of the pen describe the room and its furnishings and indicate the spatial ambience of the brooding, portly figure. Later artists who came across Rembrandt's drawings often misunderstood the significance of his "shorthand" technique, and actually spoiled precious drawings by attempting to "finish" them in a more conventional manner.

Many of Rembrandt's drawings were preliminary sketches for etchings. This graphic medium became extremely popular during the seventeenth century; in fact, during his lifetime Rembrandt's fame as etcher sometimes exceeded that as painter. Before the advent of Rembrandt, etching and engraving were regarded as similar techniques, although etching is basically more fluid. While the engraver must work hard to overcome the limitations imposed by pushing the burin directly into the resistant metal, the etcher draws with a needle on a waxed plate which is then submerged in an acid bath. More than any other artist working in the medium, Rembrandt realized the potential of the relative freedom of etching. His line is extraordinarily versatile, varying in length, intensity, and mobility. Just as he was engaged by the immediacy and intimacy of drawing, Rembrandt responded to the challenge of black and white etchings, destined to reach a very large public since hundreds of prints could be made from a single plate and the plate itself could still be reworked and printed again.

Rembrandt first began etching during the late 1620s while still in Leyden, and continued to develop the medium's expressive possibilities until the last decade of his life. The earliest efforts, like the portrait of his mother done in 1628 (Figure 13), are light, silvery, and delicate in tone, with a marked refinement of line. After his move to Amsterdam, the etchings reflect the changes in his paintings as Rembrandt continually sought to enhance the contrast of light and dark. Another significant change in his painting style during the 1640s also reverberates in the etchings. Its beginnings can be seen in a *View of Amsterdam* etched around 1640 (Figure 14), in which there is a new openness and, above all, a delicate sureness in the handling of the meshlike lines. Particularly effective is the manner in which Rembrandt has utilized the whiteness of the paper to increase the effect of atmospheric light. Everywhere there are subtle indications of space which complement the strong sense of outline; for example, the succession of windmills which gradually diminish in size and draw the viewer's eye from the right center of the composition almost to the edge of the plate mark.

The culmination of Rembrandt's experimentation with various graphic techniques came in the late 1640s and 1650s. One of the greatest etchings of this period is *Christ Healing the Sick,* or, as it is usually called, *The Hundred Guilder Print,* a title which seems to derive from a price the etching brought at auction in the seventeenth century (Figure 15). Like Rembrandt's other mature work, it departs from earlier etchings in that drypoint and burin work are combined with the etching technique. Most of the drawing has been done with an etching needle, but the burin is used in the shadowy background areas, and the vigorous drypoint needle has given a more forceful outline to the forms in the foreground.

The subject of Rembrandt's composition comes from the Gospel of Saint Matthew, which describes Christ's preaching to the multitudes and the healing of the sick who had followed him from Galilee. A crowd has gathered around Christ while others press through a passage-way to the right in an effort to reach Him. In the upper left hand corner are Pharisees, who were constantly challenging Christ with theological questions. To the immediate right of Christ, St. Peter attempts to restrain a woman who advances towards the gesturing figure of the Saviour. Just behind her one sees a well-dressed, perplexed young man, doubtless the rich man described in the gospel, who could not decide whether to forsake his inheritance in order to follow Christ and His disciples.

Rembrandt not only integrates the most important elements of the narrative, but does so in a supremely dramatic way. Appropriately, the figure of Christ dominates although

Figure 15.
Christ Healing the Sick
known as
The Hundred Guilder Print
(1648-1650)
etching, 11⅛″ x 15½″
Metropolitan Museum of Art
New York
Bequest of
Mrs. H. O. Havemeyer, 1929

each figure possesses a measure of individual character and integrity, which once more proves Rembrandt the consummate master of human emotion. Virtually all eyes look towards the Healer, and the unity of the central group is further underlined by the use of a pyramidal form with the head of Christ as its apex. Sir Kenneth Clark has discussed the manner in which Rembrandt, in this graphic masterpiece, referred once again to the drawing studies after Leonardo's *Last Supper*. For example, there is considerable similarity in the positions of the skeptical Pharisees and those of Leonardo's Apostles, and a general agreement in mood, with the comparably gentle figure of Christ set off from the busyness of the group.

One of the major factors in achieving the great sense of balance which so characterizes this work is Rembrandt's handling of light. Velvety dark tones are contrasted with the brightest and sunniest of whites. Particularly striking is the chiaroscuro on the figure of Christ: the softest shadows play over the lower half of the vertical form, while the brightness of the torso and luminous head stand out against the dark wall of the background.

Although the 1640s were both extremely productive and artistically critical years for Rembrandt, they also marked the beginning of a long period of personal tragedy. The artist's mother died in 1640. Two years later his beloved Saskia died. She had lost three children in infancy and her health had declined steadily after the birth of their son Titus. Rembrandt's melancholy was further aggravated by serious financial problems. The purchase of his fine house largely contributed to his money difficulties, but there is no question that his popularity as a portraitist had waned considerably. He had to face a great deal of competition not only from the suave and elegant style of Anthony van Dyck, but from pupils such as Ferdinand Bols and Govaert Flinck who eagerly bowed to conventional demands for straightforward likenesses, while their master maintained his independence, gave less and less importance to naturalistic effects, and concentrated on dramatic chiaroscuro.

The effect of Rembrandt's hardships upon his work was remarkable. Whereas earlier he had been concerned largely with developing a vocabulary of naturalistic forms within the context of Baroque splendor and theatricality, his work in the 1640s and 1650s displayed a greater simplicity and a sad, introspective calm. Turning again to the people and places around him for inspiration, he began to study the Jewish community of Amsterdam, etching portraits of acquaintances, such as the noted physician Ephraim Bonus, and utilizing the sketches he made in the Jewish quarter as prototypes for Biblical subjects. He began also to look at nature with a fresh eye, and to compose numerous drawings and etchings of the outskirts of Amsterdam, which provided the stimulus for later oil paintings.

Although landscapes only constitute about one-tenth of Rembrandt's total *oeuvre,* they reflect his constantly developing ideas. While most of the landscape drawings are quite spontaneous and realistic in their description of naturalistic details, the oil paintings present a grander, more idealized, or even philosophic concept of nature. In pen and wash drawings, such as *Cottages Before a Stormy Sky* (Figure 16), the dramatic sweep of nature, expressed

Figure 16.
Cottages Before a Stormy Sky (c.1641)
pen and wash in bistre and India ink
7¼″ x 9⅝″
Graphische Sammlung Albertina, Vienna

through the quickly moving sky, is played against the sturdy form of the peasant cottages Rembrandt knew so well. The area of wash in the sky and the dark, vigorous brushwork in the foreground anticipate later, more considered, atmospheric studies in oil.

During the 1640s Rembrandt also expressed affection and delight in his young son Titus (Slide 16), whom he represented in numerous drawings, etchings, and oil paintings—sometimes as himself, but often in various biblical scenes as the young Joseph, or Christ, or the prophet Daniel. With increasing frequency Rembrandt began to utilize another model, Hendrickje Stoffels, who had come to his house about 1645 as a servant girl, and subsequently became his intimate and devoted companion.

The daughter of a simple soldier, Hendrickje was completely different from Saskia. She had none of the latter's refinement or feminine charm, but from the artist's many portraits of her the warmth and good humor of her character are as apparent as Rembrandt's deep affection. Although their relationship was never legalized because the terms of Saskia's will did not permit him to remarry, Hendrickje doesn't seem to have suffered greatly from the lack of a formal marriage, despite the fact that members of the Reformed Church Council repeatedly called her in for interviews, and punished her "sinfulness" by excluding her from Holy Communion.

When Rembrandt's great financial failure came in the mid-1650s, Hendrickje and young Titus joined forces to protect the painter from numerous creditors. After his personal property had been liquidated at auction, they formed a partnership as art dealers and, in 1660, made Rembrandt their employee. In return for their support, the painter promised to give them all he produced. A fragment of this document illustrates the pathetic manner in which this arrangement allowed Rembrandt to salvage at least the earnings of his future work:

> . . . Further, both parties have each brought all they possess into the partnership, and Titus van Rijn in particular has brought his baptismal gifts, his savings, his personal earnings, and other belongings he still possesses. All that either party earns in the future is to be held in common. According to his company's proceedings, each is to receive half of the profits and bear half of the losses . . .
>
> But as they require some help in their business, and as no one is more capable than the aforementioned Rembrandt van Rijn, the contracting parties agree that he shall live with them and receive free board and lodging and be excused of housekeeping matters and rent on condition that he will, as much as possible, promote their interests and try to make profits for the company; to this he agrees and promises.

Although Rembrandt's popularity in Holland was now at its lowest point, historical data, preserved in the archives of the Ruffo family, verifies the impression that his reputation remained firmly established in Italy. In 1652 Don Antonio Ruffo, a Sicilian nobleman who

Figure 17. *Aristotle Contemplating the Bust of Homer* (1653)
oil on canvas, 56½" x 53¾"
Metropolitan Museum of Art, New York
purchased with special funds and gifts of friends of the Museum, 1961

owned a sizable collection of paintings, wrote Rembrandt to request a "philosopher," the *Aristotle Contemplating the Bust of Homer*, finished in 1653 (Figure 17). Eight years later Ruffo received an *Alexander the Great*, which apparently displeased him because he complained to Rembrandt that it was merely a head filled out on four sides to make a half-length figure. The correspondence between painter and client also refers to a third picture of Homer, which, after some changes, was accepted by Ruffo in 1663.

During the ten or eleven years of association with Rembrandt, the Italian collector decided to augment Rembrandt's group of philosophers with works by contemporary Italians, and approached Guercino and Mattia Preti. In a letter designating requirements for the painting, Ruffo requested that Guercino work in his earlier, tenebrous manner which he felt would be more compatible with the deep chiaroscuro of Rembrandt's *Aristotle*. Guercino's reply provided a generous testimonial to the abilities of his Dutch contemporary:

> As for the half-figure by Rembrandt which has come into your hands, it cannot be other than complete perfection because I have seen various works of his in prints which have come to our region. They are very beautiful in execution; engraved with good taste and done in a fine manner; so that one can assume that his work in color is likewise of complete exquisiteness and perfection. I sincerely esteem him as a great artist.

Unlike Guercino's companion piece, Rembrandt's Aristotle does not engage the spectator, but remains absorbed in his own thoughtful speculation. The philosopher's right hand rests gently on the head of the great poet he so admired, the curve of his sleeve linking them in spirit as well as in composition. Among the items in Rembrandt's collection was a cast of a portrait bust of Homer, which we can assume he used as a model for this work. The moving calm of the painting contrasts strikingly with Rembrandt's earlier conception of mythological or historical personalities. Controlled coloring contributes to the solemn dignity: the sumptuous gold of Aristotle's chain glitters against the simple black and white of his gown, while warm, golden-brown shadows, illuminating the face of Aristotle and the bust of the poet, gradually darken into the background.

One of Rembrandt's most magnificent compositions and a work which underlines his compassion and inherent tenderness is *The Jewish Bride* (Figure 18), dating from the mid-1660s and representative of his last style. Ever since the title was given to the painting in the early nineteenth century, scholars have attempted to provide a fuller explanation of its subject. Although Rembrandt probably painted a bridal couple from life, the quiet solemnity of the gestures and mood suggest a deeper, more symbolic meaning. Perhaps, in this tribute to love, Rembrandt wished to represent a bridal couple in the guise of a famed Old Testament pair, such as Esther and Ahasuerus, Tobias and Sarah, Jacob and Rachel, or Isaac and Rebecca. The beautifully painted figures, shown in three-quarter length, stand

Figure 18.
Portrait of a Bridal Pair
known as *The Jewish Bride* (mid-1660s)
oil on canvas, 48″ x 65½″
Rijksmuseum, Amsterdam

apart from their almost murky surroundings, and the light seems to radiate from within the figures rather than from any external source. The costumes are dazzling, but it is the gestures of the young couple which capture and hold the viewer's imagination. The *Jewish Bride* marks one of the high points in Rembrandt's artistic career, and possibly the culmination of his continuous striving to combine the universal and the personal in a work of art.

The decade of the *Jewish Bride* was perhaps the hardest period of Rembrandt's life. In 1663 Hendrickje died, leaving the aging and ailing painter in the care of his twenty-three-year-old son Titus. In 1668 Titus, who also maintained the family business, married the daughter of a silversmith. A few months later he died suddenly, leaving Rembrandt the responsibility of caring for his half-sister Cornelia whom Hendrickje had borne in 1654. His final self-portrait, done the year of his death, 1669, provides moving testimony of Rembrandt's final sorrows. The painting, as fragile as the painter's physical and psychological condition, is wistfully sad and manifests the infirmities of old age: the artist's features seem flabby, his usually expressive eyes appear vacant and lack that intense vitality which had literally burst from his earlier canvases.

Some of Rembrandt's biographers have tended to emphasize the loneliness of his later life, although it is quite clear that he had been deeply and happily involved with his family, and that his retirement from the more frivolous and purely social aspects of Amsterdam public life had been, at least partly, a matter of personal preference. Many seventeenth-century writers criticized the painter for not cultivating associations with poets and other educated people and for apparently preferring the company of common or even low people. Houbraken, for example, commented that "in the autumn of his life Rembrandt kept company mostly with common people and such as practiced art," while the fastidious classicist Baldinucci maintained that "the ugly and plebian face with which Rembrandt was ill-favored was accompanied by untidy and dirty clothes, since it was his custom, when working, to wipe his brushes on himself and to do other things of a similar nature."

However unfair or exaggerated the judgment of his critics may seem now, there is no question that Rembrandt was a man of extraordinary independence who cared little for convention and whose driving obsession was his work. Unlike his great contemporary Van Dyck, Rembrandt had no desire to court or flatter possible patrons with elegant portraits or idealized religious subjects. His strength lay in the powerful sensibility and compassion he expressed through the many paintings, etchings, and drawings.

Despite considerable harsh criticism, Rembrandt's reputation as a painter of international renown was established by the 1640s and persisted throughout his life. His paintings were collected by the Stuart kings of England and the Medici of Florence; in 1667 Cosimo de' Medici, Grand Duke of Tuscany, even visited the artist's studio. During the last decade of his life, although his great popularity in Amsterdam had declined significantly, Rembrandt still received important large commissions such as the great *Syndics of the Drapers' Guild* (Slide 19).

During the final phase of his artistic development, Rembrandt evolved a style which transcended the visual realism of his earlier work. However, his understanding and appreciation of the human condition, of its inherent fragility and melancholy, gives universal appeal to all his work, while his ability to look within and yet beyond himself invests his art with an implicity personal warmth unequaled by any other master.

SELECTED BIBLIOGRAPHY

Benesch, Otto, *The Drawings of Rembrandt* (6 vols.), Phaidon Press, London, 1954-57.

Boon, K. G., *Rembrandt: The Complete Etchings,* Thames and Hudson, London, 1963.

Clark, Kenneth, *Rembrandt and the Italian Renaissance,* New York University Press, 1966.

Gerson, H., *Rembrandt Paintings,* Reynal and Company, New York, 1968.

Rosenberg, Jakob, *Rembrandt: Life and Work,* Phaidon Press, London, 1964.

COMMENTARY ON THE SLIDES

COMMENTARY ON THE SLIDES

1: LAUGHING SELF-PORTRAIT (1629-30), oil on copper
6⅛″ x 4″, Mauritshuis, The Hague

The years following Rembrandt's return from Amsterdam to Leyden were extraordinarily active ones. Establishing himself as an independent master at nineteen, he set out to make a name for himself as a painter of portraits and of Old Testament subjects. As part of a continuing effort to improve his descriptive powers, the painter frequently turned to his own features. Between the years 1629 and 1631, he produced a large number of paintings, as well as a series of small etchings (Figure 1), in which he reproduced a wide range of facial expressions: surprise, anger, and very often, good-humored laughter. In this self-portrait Rembrandt has attempted to capture and project a fleeting, spontaneous emotion. The right side of his homely face is bathed in strong light; his bulbous nose fairly glows with a vitality that is matched by the metallic glitter of the military collar the painter has borrowed for the occasion.

In this and in other self-portraits of the same period, we can observe Rembrandt exploring bold contrasts of light and dark in order to achieve a maximum degree of pictorial animation. However, the somewhat frozen quality of the exaggerated open mouth and staring eyes appears self-conscious and in no way prepares us for the penetrating characterizations that emerge from the painter's mature portraits.

2: THE ANATOMY LESSON OF DOCTOR NICOLAAS TULP (1632)
oil on canvas, 66¾″ x 85¼″, Mauritshuis, The Hague

The painting of portraits proved to be most profitable for seventeenth-century Dutch painters. While artists in England, France, and Spain had to rely largely on the more limited royal or aristocratic patronage, Holland's large and prosperous middle class seemed most anxious to have themselves portrayed in paint. In addition to individual and family portraits, Rembrandt was called upon to produce official group portraits for various societies and guilds. Sometimes as many as thirty figures might be represented in these painted *tours de force* and, since his fee was split evenly among them, the artist was expected to do justice to each individual. In his lifetime Rembrandt produced four of these large masterworks: two depicted anatomy lessons held by the Surgeons' Guild of Amsterdam; one showed a large company of militia men on their way to a shooting match (Slide 10); and the last immortalized the sober board members of the Drapers' Guild (Slide 19).

In *The Anatomy Lesson of Doctor Tulp* we are present at the rare occasion of the dissection of a corpse before a large paying audience. The seven younger doctors follow the words of the formally dressed master surgeon with varying degrees of interest. The careful, pyramidal grouping of the figures creates a remarkable degree of coherence, and yet the individuality of each sitter is manifest. The faces of the men and their ruffled white collars stand out strikingly against their dark costumes and the brownish-gray walls. Instead of merely describing an event, Rembrandt's versatile handling of light and dark accents lends the work an aura of high excitement.

3: THE DESCENT FROM THE CROSS (1633), oil on panel
35¼″ x 25¾″, Alte Pinakothek, Munich

Of all the religious works produced by Rembrandt during the thirties, the series of the Passion, done for Prince Frederick Henry of Orange, is by far the finest. When he accepted the Prince's invitation to undertake the series, Rembrandt must have been well aware that any *Descent from the Cross* would be compared with the powerful altarpiece of the same scene which Rubens had executed twenty years before in Antwerp. In fact, Rembrandt borrowed freely from the Flemish painter by utilizing the same sagging, downward movement, while slightly modifying the positions of the men who lower Christ's body. However, Rembrandt significantly altered the busyness of Rubens' compositional scheme by removing the three mourning women from the central action and placing them in the lower left-hand corner. In addition, he strengthened the physical and psychological rapport of the main figures by focusing the strongest concentration of light—indeed, virtually the only light in the painting—on the winding sheet which frames the body of Christ. Also, unlike Rubens whose respect for aesthetic ideals of the Italian Renaissance influenced his rendering of perfect human forms, Rembrandt felt free to employ the stark realism that was to mark so much of his later work. The pathetic body of Christ sags heavily, emphasizing the "deadness" the painter wished to convey. The twisting of the head, which falls limply to the side, and the otherwise inelegant positioning of the body are a far cry from the serenity and classical proportions so prominent in Renaissance versions of the same theme.

One impressive aspect of the painting is the manner in which the viewer actually feels that the people depicted are not only present but truly involved in the action. In several letters to his friend and sponsor Constantin Huygens, Rembrandt revealed some of the profound religious sentiments that he experienced while working on the Passion series, and expressed his desire to communicate "the greatest and most innate emotion." The sincere feelings of the painter shine through the faces of the various participants in this great tragedy, and it is not surprising to learn that the figure in blue on the ladder, who gazes so intently at the dead Christ, is modelled after the artist himself.

4: THE RAPE OF GANYMEDE (1635), oil on canvas, 67¼″ x 51¼″
Staatliche Kunstsammlungen, Dresden

Although he had attended Leyden's Latin School where the curriculum included the reading of Cicero, Virgil, Horace, and Ovid, Rembrandt's interest in mythological and other classicizing subjects was rather limited. During his formative years with Peter Lastman in Amsterdam, he developed a brief fondness for classical themes, but after the mid-thirties, these subjects virtually disappeared from his repertoire.

One outstanding mythological subject taken from Ovid's *Metamorphoses, The Rape of Ganymede,* illustrates the young painter's struggle to produce a bold new interpretation of a time-worn classical theme. Instead of depicting the beautiful youth who inspired the cruel and lecherous god Zeus to assume the form of an eagle and carry him off to Mount Olympus, Rembrandt has daringly substituted a chubby, whining child, whose frightened reaction to the rude assault is clearly visible. The impression the work creates with its startling chiaroscuro is one of initial surprise and subsequent amusement. As Caravaggio had attempted to redefine or refashion classical personages such as Bacchus, Amor, or Narcissus forty years before, Rembrandt's uncompromising naturalism prompted the translation of elegant or poetic themes into a frank and downright earthy idiom.

5: SASKIA AS FLORA (1635), oil on canvas, 48⅝″ x 38⅜″
The National Gallery, London

Nowhere is the fanciful or romantic aspect of Rembrandt's style better reflected than in the many portraits he painted of his wife, Saskia van Uylenburgh. That he adored his elegant and well-born wife is clear from the fact that she came to represent the female ideal in his religious and mythological paintings. Saskia is seen in many guises—Delilah, Bellona, Minerva—but nowhere is she more handsomely depicted than in the allegorical portrait of Flora, the Roman goddess of Spring.

In representing a contemporary person in the guise of a classical deity, Rembrandt was following an established convention of Baroque painting. However, the young painter seems to have gone somewhat overboard in an effort to give the painting a haughty and eloquent air. At times we become so dazzled by the textural variations of the costume, the vine-covered sword, and the cluster of flowers, that we find it difficult to concentrate on the broad but handsome face of the golden-haired goddess. Indeed, the overly rich setting and the numerous props seem to overwhelm the personality of the sitter.

It is interesting to note that in much later treatments of the same theme, where the artist used his servant and mistress Hendricjke Stoffels as model, the approach was quite different. Instead of bombast, he produced quiet, solemn works which transcend the somewhat homelier features of the sitter.

6: THE BLINDING OF SAMSON (1636), oil on canvas, 93" x 119"
Städelsches Kunstinstitut, Frankfurt am Main

The many paintings Rembrandt produced during the 1630s combine extraordinary force and drama. Easily the most brutal of all the artist's compositions, *The Blinding of Samson* contains elements that recall both the paintings of the early Baroque master Caravaggio and those of Rembrandt's Flemish contemporary Peter Paul Rubens. Caravaggio had painted a similar theme, *The Martyrdom of St. Matthew,* some thirty-five years before, and Rembrandt's diagonally foreshortened figure of Samson and use of sprawling and fleeing figures as foils for the strongly illuminated victim suggest that he had studied carefully the works of Caravaggio's Dutch followers, Gerrit Honthorst and Hendrick Terbrugghen (Figure 3).

Whereas Rubens had chosen to represent Samson struggling with his captors, Rembrandt depicts the actual putting out of the titan's eyes. The strong diagonal line of the outstretched halberd initially directs the viewer's gaze to the contorted, blood-splattered face of Samson, where it rests briefly before journeying upward and outward to the figure of the triumphant Delilah fleeing with the shorn hair of the deceived hero. The combination of interlocking diagonals and swirling circular movement, almost life-size figures, and a remarkable range of colors, as well as the mixture of violence and pathos, mark the painting as one of the most outspokenly theatrical of Rembrandt's works.

7: A POLISH NOBLEMAN (1637), oil on panel, 38⅛" x 26"
National Gallery of Art, Washington, D.C., Andrew Mellon Collection

It is quite likely that this portrait of a "Polish nobleman" is an example of one of the many fanciful representations of Slavs and Orientals the young painter produced during the 1630s. The studied, almost theatrical, aspect of the rich furs and gilttering golden chains lead one to believe that the artist has literally invented the Slavic aristocrat by dressing a homely man in one of the splendid costumes he usually kept in his studio.

Despite its clear theatricality, the painting documents Rembrandt's rather impressive skills, for he has clearly mastered the various textures shown—from the metal of the chains and the head of the cane to the soft, cushy velvet and the silken fur. The artist has fully realized the plasticity of the human form and has begun to utilize light, not only for purposes of modeling and textural definition, but in order to create a mood or psychological ambience. The glittering golds and warm reds, which are employed so effectively here, are enhanced by the subtle half-tones in the shadowy background.

8: THE STONE BRIDGE (1637-38), oil on canvas, 11½″ x 16¾″
Rijksmuseum, Amsterdam

While landscapes had always figured prominently in the backgrounds of religious and historical subjects that were popular during the time when the country was still Catholic, they did not emerge as an independent and important genre of painting until Holland became a free, independent, and largely Protestant country in the seventeenth century. Then landscapes were so sought after that various types or categories were established: some painters, for example, dealt only with marine views; others produced city views; still others only winter scenes.

Rembrandt's interest in landscape developed during the second half of the 1630s and lasted for about seventeen years. Although landscapes make up no more than one tenth of the artist's total *oeuvre,* they reflect the same wide range of attitudes and technical development that we encounter in his other types of painting. Some of his landscapes are visionary or fantastic, others almost prosaically descriptive, while a few transcend the limitations imposed by the genre and constitute moving philosophic statements about nature.

The Stone Bridge dates from Rembrandt's earliest landscape period when he deliberately sought to depict nature at her most dramatic. A favorite device of his at this time was the juxtaposition of threatening darkish clouds with an almost eerie golden light; thus, the great sweep of sky seems to overwhelm the small bridge and the fragile boats that ply the waters of the stream. Just as Rembrandt's portraits and religious paintings of the same period strove to convey the dramatic urgency of a scene, this painting, with its violently animated forms, conveys a similar sense of Baroque theatricality.

9: REMBRANDT'S MOTHER (1639), oil on panel, 31¼" x 24¼"
Kunsthistorisches Museum, Vienna

If we compare the portraits painted in Amsterdam by Rembrandt in the 1630s with those of his immediate predecessors or competitors, we can observe that the painter's work must have struck many as being slightly unorthodox in that it did not present the studied, sometimes painful draughtsmanship and fussy detailing that characterized the work of other successful portraitists.

While Rembrandt's early portraits reveal more concern with costume details than do his later works, they already establish a fundamentally different appreciation of the character and inner life of the sitter, an appreciation conspicuously absent from the portraits done by his contemporaries. A number of portraits of the artist's mother underscore Rembrandt's gentle understanding of the elderly and his respect and affection for their worth as individuals. In a more fanciful mood, Rembrandt had depicted his mother as the prophetess Hannah (Figure 5), thus affirming the deep religious convictions and piety of the old woman. A year before her death he produced this portrait, an intimate and touching study of a frail figure leaning heavily on a cane, her sad, downcast eyes suggesting that she is virtually waiting for death. Where the fanciful portrayal of 1631 was expansive—rich in textures, dramatic plays of light, and definitely atmospheric—this painting is economical and spare. The light is confined to the face of the old woman, and the curving pyramid of her headdress forces the viewer's eye to dwell on the aged, suffering face and folded hands.

10: THE NIGHT WATCH (The Militia Company of Captain Frans Banning Cocq) (1642), oil on canvas, 143" x 172", Rijksmuseum, Amsterdam

Rembrandt's largest and most celebrated group portrait, the so-called *Night Watch,* is also one of his most controversial paintings. The popular title given to the work is misleading and inaccurate. When the painting was removed from its wartime storage place in 1945 and properly cleaned, it was apparent that despite the strong chiaroscuro that marks the work, the action took place during the day. In fact, the militia men are not going off to war, but are assembling to attend one of the frequent shooting contests that enabled them to socialize as well as to practice their marksmanship.

Whereas Rembrandt had achieved unity in his *Anatomy Lesson of Dr. Tulp* (Slide 2) by playing off the group of students against the somewhat detached figure of the lecturing surgeon, the two commanding officers of the shooting company are part of a large, sprawling composition which has no single unity or focal point. It is the color or tonal contrasts that pull the painting together: the yellow of the lieutenant's uniform is repeated in the costume of a little girl seen in the crowd, and in the flag held aloft; the red of the captain's sash is echoed in uniforms, scarves, and in the drum to the right. Although the warm, golden glow that resulted from the juxtaposition of the reds and yellows proved to be extremely effective in Rembrandt's paintings of the forties and fifties, the viewer still faces the problem of trying to integrate the seemingly unrelated clusters of figures.

Instead of choosing to represent the company in a more formal situation, namely, marching or standing at attention, the artist has shown them in the process of assembling. The drum rolls, a dog barks in answer to it, while various other figures hoist their weapons, or examine them. In the midst of the activity and noise, a little girl with a dead game-bird hanging from her belt scurries through a golden opening in the crowd. She carries in her hand a silver cup—possibly a trophy for the winner of the shooting contest—yet her presence still strikes the viewer as odd. The fact is that on examining her face one sees distinct resemblance to Rembrandt's wife, Saskia, who died the year the painting was finished.

The zig-zagging directional movement of the painting, resulting from the use of strong, diagonal lines, creates a sense of vitality which probably struck some of Rembrandt's contemporaries as unorthodox. In addition, the fact that the eighteen members of the company were not individually and instantaneously recognizable and that Rembrandt even added anonymous and unrelated figures, such as the little girl, made the painting both controversial and puzzling.

11: THE SUPPER AT EMMAUS (1648), oil on panel, 26¾" x 25½"
Louvre, Paris

One of Rembrandt's favorite religious themes was the supper at Emmaus, wherein the resurrected Christ revealed Himself to two of His disciples. While earlier representations of this theme (including one painted by Rembrandt in 1629) had stressed the miraculous nature of the event and exaggerated the surprised or frightened reactions of Christ's companions, this mature conception emphasized the piety and serenity of the extraordinary moment.

The absolute clarity and simplicity of the composition—the virtually bare, altar-like table, the near symmetry of the figure grouping, and the restraint of the gestures—lend the work an almost ceremonial quality. The natural, fading light of the room and the supernatural light that emanates from the figure of Christ merge and create an ambience which seems both ideal and real.

By far the most compelling aspect of the work is the manner in which the gentle, passive figure of Christ imposes Himself not only on the consciousness of the disciples but on the viewer as well. Rarely has a painter projected an article of religious faith with as much quiet conviction as this.

12: RIVER VALLEY WITH RUINS (c. 1650), oil on panel, 26½″ x 34¼″
Staatliche Kunstsammlungen, Kassel

While Rembrandt favored the momentary aspects of nature in his early landscapes, the works produced in the late 1640s and 1650s are representative of a change in attitude which can be observed in his work as a whole. Although the painter still populates his landscape with ruined castles, old mills, and relatively small figures, something has happened to the way in which he sees nature. This painting is less of a fragment than *The Stone Bridge* (Slide 8); it has more breadth, and possesses a grandeur and monumentality which results, in part, from a different handling of color.

Whereas previously Rembrandt had relied on clashing contrasts of light and dark, he now employs a more diffused, benign light; the gentle blues and whites of the sky will not be violated by the darkening cloud. Moreover, one senses in the work a stability and calm—visible both in the architecture and in the structure of nature itself—which approaches the grandeur of the great seventeenth-century classical landscape tradition initiated in Italy by Annibale Carracci and developed by the Northern artist Adam Elsheimer.

13: BATHSHEBA (1654), oil on canvas, 56″ x 56″
Louvre, Paris

By the time he painted this picture, Rembrandt had already executed several other versions of the same subject with the sumptuous colors and flamboyant theatricality that marked his more Baroque style. This work displays a new quiet, a new humanity and, above all, a subtle psychological awareness that was previously absent from the other compositions.

Rembrandt has chosen to show Bathsheba in an attitude of incredible intimacy and meditation. Her bath is finished, and while her maidservant dries her feet she contemplates the significance of the letter she holds in her hand. The message from King David is, of course, an invitation to come to his bedchamber—an invitation which would mean adultery, since Bathsheba was married. The conflict that must have beset her and the knowledge that betrayal of her husband would certainly lead to suffering can be seen in the melancholy inclination of Bathsheba's head and in the downcast eyes.

The amazing simplicity of the composition and the basic naturalism of the female nude belie the complexity of the painting and the difficulties of the period in which it was painted. The model for the figure of Bathsheba was Hendrickje Stoffels, Rembrandt's servant and mistress, who bore the painter a daughter during the year the painting was completed, and was herself severely chastised by the local church council for her illegal union with Rembrandt.

14: WOMAN BATHING IN A STREAM (1654), oil on panel, 24⁵⁄₁₆″ x 18¼″
The National Gallery, London

One of the most striking things about this painting is its size: compared with most of Rembrandt's work it is tiny, measuring only about twenty-four by eighteen inches. In addition, the vivid and lively brushwork, manifest especially in the chalky white of the nightshirt and the vigorous brushes of gold and red which indicate the woman's garment resting on the bank, underline the freshness and spontaneity of the situation. In fact, the painting is an affectionate souvenir of Hendrickje, who served, as Saskia had previously done, as model for many paintings of the fifties and sixties.

It has been suggested that this lively little sketch may have been a preliminary study for a biblical subject, possibly *Bathsheba* or *Susanna and the Elders*. Whatever its ultimate purpose, the painting clearly illustrates that Rembrandt was constantly sharpening his perceptions, constantly developing his draughtsmanship and refining his mastery of light. Like the many drawing studies of females reclining or bathing, this painting testifies to the artist's unswerving commitment to visual truth.

15: THE SLAUGHTERED OX (1655), oil on panel, 37″ x 26½″
Louvre, Paris

Two versions of the painting exist: the one under discussion and another work in the Glasgow Art Gallery. Both paintings include the figure of a woman, but whereas here she is depicted peering at the slain animal from the doorway, in the Glasgow work she sweeps the floor behind the hanging carcass.

The history of this painting is rather interesting and indicative of changing attitudes toward Rembrandt's work and toward subjects of a stark or brutal nature. The torn and battered corpse of the ox must have repelled nineteenth-century collectors, because the painting was sold to the Louvre about one hundred years ago for the modest sum of five thousand francs.

Although the painting must be classified as a still life, the overwhelming presence of the carcass and the strange regard of the woman produce an unusual combination of naturalism and mysticism. Where the woman in the Glasgow *Slaughtered Ox* accepts the ordinary or everyday nature of her job, here she acts almost as a witness contemplating an executed victim—perhaps reflecting the painter's changing attitude toward his life and his work.

16: TITUS AT HIS DESK (1655), oil on canvas, 30¼″ x 24¾″
Boymans-van Beuningen Museum, Rotterdam

Rembrandt's son was born in 1642, the year that his wife Saskia died. During the fifties and sixties, along with Hendrickje Stoffels, the boy was one of his father's favorite models. It is safe to assume that the sad circumstances of Titus' birth drew Rembrandt even closer to his son, and the many portraits that date from the mid-fifties until Titus' premature death in 1668 testify to the father's deep affection.

While Titus served as model for the youthful Tobias, the Daniels, and the Josephs that Rembrandt produced at this time, the artist's most touching likenesses are the intimate studies of the boy reading or drawing at his desk. Undoubtedly the earliest of these portrait types is this work which shows the boy deep in contemplation—his drawing pen in one hand, his ink container dangling from the other. Although the face is that of a child—a child who already resembles his father—the mood suggested by the serious dark eyes is distinctly serious and mature. The forthright gaze seems to be addressed to the viewer and establishes an immediate rapport with him.

In this painting Rembrandt creates amazingly subtle color harmonies. The golden-brown hair of the boy, his dullish red cap and sleeves, and the green coat are all reflected in the tonality of the desk, wherein each color is carefully employed to stabilize the whole composition.

17: JOSEPH ACCUSED BY POTIPHAR'S WIFE (1655), oil on canvas, 41⅝″ x 38½″
National Gallery of Art, Washington, D.C., Andrew Mellon Collection

In his search for mastery of dramatic subjects, Rembrandt returned to certain themes again and again. Occasionally he painted successive treatments of the same subject within a very short period of time. This is true of *Joseph and Potiphar's Wife,* of which he produced two versions in 1655.

The Old Testament subject certainly offered the maximum possibility for dramatic expressiveness, and Rembrandt has responded to the high drama of the theme. The wife of Potiphar, the pharaoh's Captain of the Guard, is unjustly accusing Joseph, his slave, of having made advances to her. The central protagonist is the treacherous wife; Joseph stands passively at her right, and Potiphar, splendidly dressed in exotic satins and oriental turban, listens intently to her lies. The villainess of the piece radiates with false innocence. The strong, golden spotlight that plays on her face and declaiming hands falls across the pillows of the bed and rests gently on the shoulders of the victim, Joseph. The magical reds and golds—so dear to Rembrandt—convey the luxury of the setting and, at the same time, force the viewer to consider the purely painterly values of the work as well as to admire its narrative power.

18: THE DENIAL OF PETER (1660), oil on canvas, 60½″ x 66½″
Rijksmuseum, Amsterdam

Rembrandt's later religious paintings, like his later portraits, reveal an increasing concern with the inner life of human beings. The self-portraits executed in the 1660s show the effect of the artist's day-to-day sufferings and express the strength of character that enabled him to overcome or transcend the circumstances of his life and create great works of art. The religious paintings also tell us a great deal about Rembrandt's character. Perhaps because of his own appreciation of the frailties of the human condition, Rembrandt chose biblical subjects, such as the *Denial of Peter,* which illustrate the inner conflict that is the inevitable result of betrayal of one's convictions. Peter is confronted by the problem of whether to deny Christ and save his own life or acknowledge Him and face imprisonment or death. As Christ predicted, he chooses life, but the personal suffering he must endure as a result of his choice is already visible on the troubled face.

All dramatic attention is focused on Peter's face, which is illuminated by the intense light of a candle held by a woman. The Apostle's surprise, sorrow, and fear are combined in his expression, but something of his innate dignity is salvaged by his priestly stance and gesture. Rembrandt does not let us forget that this is after all the man of whom Christ said: ". . . And upon this rock I will build my church; and the gates of hell shall not prevail against it." (Matthew 16:18).

In choosing to emphasize the dramatic confrontation of the challenged Apostle with the questioning and grim soldiers and the unbelieving woman, Rembrandt has created not only a powerful religious drama, but also one with subtle psychological undertones. The raised arm of the woman and the gesturing fingers of St. Peter lead the viewer's gaze to the upper right-hand corner of the picture where the small, backward-glancing face of a man is caught in a sliver of light. The face is that of the captive Christ, who witnesses the realization of His warning to Peter: "Before the cock crow, thou shalt deny me thrice' (Luke 22: 61-62).

19: THE SYNDICS OF THE DRAPERS' GUILD (1662), oil on canvas, 75¼″ x 110″
Rijksmuseum, Amsterdam

The last of Rembrandt's official group portraits bears two signatures: clearly visible on the wall above the wainscoting is the date 1661, while the less legible 1662 appears on the table covering. One may conclude from this that the picture consumed more time than the painter had initially intended, or that he made some changes or additions after the first date. X-rays have revealed that the hatless servant who appears in the center of the group previously had been placed to the extreme right of the merchants. Perhaps Rembrandt moved the figure after deciding that its original position adversely affected the balance of the composition.

Certainly the work displays a high degree of symmetry and, as Jakob Rosenberg observed, "breathes a tranquility that is rare in Rembrandt's late works." Unlike the *Night Watch* (Slide 10), where the unconventional diagonals of crisscrossing muskets and halberds create an atmosphere of almost breathtaking excitement, the meeting of the board of governors of the drapers' guild is characterized by strong and tidy vertical and horizontal accents, which lend the proceedings an air of stability. Adhering to the prevailing conventions of this type of portraiture, the artist has shown the Board in what is probably a regular meeting or conference. The sober business discussion appears to have been interrupted by the arrival of an additional person, but as that person's identity cannot be determined, the viewer is left with the impression that he is the disturber, and that the syndics turn or rise to face him. In this manner Rembrandt has established a remarkable and active rapport between sitters and spectator.

But apart from that, what impresses us is the psychological depth of the individual portraits. With great tact Rembrandt managed to indicate the importance of the chief officer (the man who is seated directly in front of the open book and whose face is bathed in the strongest light), while not sacrificing the dignity or importance of the other board members. Seen against the beautifully muted red-orange of the table covering, these shrewd, industrious sons of Holland emerge as compassionate and enlightened human beings. The golden light that fills their board room recalls the world outside, a bustling active world of which these men are an important part.

20: SELF-PORTRAIT (1669), oil on canvas, 33⅞" x 27¾"
The National Gallery, London

Until this painting was recently cleaned, it was thought to be somewhat earlier than the date which emerged from underneath the dirt and varnish—1669. It is surely one of the last self-portraits done by the artist, and it suggests that he was ready to face the difficulties of his life and even the threat of death with equanimity and something of wry humor. Unlike earlier portraits in which the artist lingered lovingly over rich costume details, the garment here is of secondary importance. The composition is straightforward: a half-length figure in three-quarter view silhouetted against a greenish-yellow wall. Brushstrokes are summary, details scarcely visible, so that the viewer is literally forced into a concentration on the features of the artist.

Rembrandt's gaze suggests a curious blend of smugness and whimsy, as though he had just delivered a witty line and was assessing its effect on his listener. That Rembrandt was capable of making brusque or even coarse remarks has been recorded in various memoirs and reminiscences—including those of his critic the Italian art historian Filippo Baldinucci. In any event, what seems likely is that the painter possessed a sort of gallows humor, which at times was directed at himself as well as others.